WALL STREET
WIT & WISDOM

WALL STREET
WIT & WISDOM

Compiled and edited
by Robert H. Thomas

Marbo Enterprises
Dallas, Texas

Copyright © 1996 by Robert H. Thomas

Published by: Marbo Enterprises, 10031 Ferndale Rd., Dallas, Texas 75238
Cover design by: Robert Kimmerle

Quantity discounts are available on bulk purchases of this book for gifts, educational purposes or fund raising. For information contact: Marbo Enterprises, PO Box 550547, Dallas, Texas 75355-0547 or call (214) 340-2147 / fax (214) 341-7081.

Library of Congress Catalog Card Number 95-080838

WALL STREET WIT & WISDOM
Compiled and edited by Robert H. Thomas

ISBN 0-9649201-0-7

Printed in the United States of America

INTRODUCTION

WALL STREET is much more than, as one cynic put it, "a thoroughfare that begins in a graveyard and ends in a river." Rather, Wall Street is the heart of corporate finance in the U.S. and symbolic of investing in the stock market. For many investors, it has proven to be a street paved with gold — while others have truly experienced a 'nightmare on Wall Street.'

Scores of books and magazine articles have been written over the years detailing how to get rich quick by playing the stock market using a variety of strategies and gimmicks. The truth is, there are no shortcuts and you will not outsmart the market — for very long. But it is very possible to create substantial wealth by investing in the stocks of some of the great companies in America.

Warren Buffett, one of the richest men in America today, accumulated his tremendous wealth solely by being a savvy and patient investor — not from reading his horoscope or deciphering squiggles on a chart.

WALL STREET WIT & WISDOM includes quotes from leading investment gurus such as Buffett, Peter Lynch, George Soros and many others, along with axioms, one-liners and cartoons all about investing on Wall Street. Hopefully, you will be entertained and amused by the *wit* — but more importantly, you should become wealthier and wiser from the *wisdom*.

To my wonderful wife, Martha and our four
terrific kids, Deni, Missy, Rob and Blair.

> Never confuse brilliance on your part with a bull market.

- ➤ A watched stock never boils.

- ➤ Markets always go to extremes.

- ➤ Bull markets climb a wall of fear.

➤ *"Only buy something that you'd be perfectly happy to hold if the market shut down for 10 years."*

— Warren Buffett

➢ Nobody rings a bell when a bull market is over.

➤ *"My biggest winners continue to be stocks I've held for three and even four years."*

— Peter Lynch

➤ *"The intelligent investor is likely to need considerable will power to keep from following the crowd."*

— Benjamin Graham

➤ As a bull market begins to peak, sell the stock that has gone up the *most* — it will drop the fastest. Sell the stock that has gone up the *least* — it didn't go up, so it must go down.

➤ The easiest way to go broke is being right *too* soon.

➤ When market optimism is really frothy, stocks seem to be discounting not only the future — but even the *hereafter*.

➤ *How* the market reacts to bad news is more important than the news itself.

➤ Why buy stock of laggard companies hoping for a turn-around, when there are plenty of stocks already heading in the right direction.

➤ *"Don't gamble. Take all your savings and buy a good stock, and hold it till it goes up, then sell it. If it don't go up, don't buy it."*

— Will Rogers

➤ Stock gains are determined by the *growth* of earnings and dividends.

➤ Bailing out of a good stock, with the idea of jumping back in later, is how most investors get burned.

➤ If you're depending on hope and prayer — it's time to get out.

➢ Don't be deluded, a loss is a loss — whether on paper or actual.

➢ You might be right about where the market is going — but you have no idea where it will go after that.

"According to my calculations, the stock market should go up, down, up, down, up, down, up, down, up, down, then up."

➤ Markets are never wrong — personal opinions are often wrong.

➤ When selecting a stock to buy, select the one you think you will never have a reason to sell.

➤ *"The chief losses to investors come from the purchase of low-quality securities at times of favorable business conditions."*

— Benjamin Graham

➤ *"There will always be bull markets followed by bear markets followed by bull markets."*

— John Templeton

➤ *"I don't know what the seven wonders of the world are, but I do know the eighth — compound interest."*

— Baron Rothschild

➢ More stocks double than go
to zero.

➤ *"Great companies bought at great
prices should be like great friends —
you don't drop them precipitously."*

— Shelby Davis

➢ Never buy a stock just after a significant rise or sell one just after a significant drop.

➢ Don't buy the sympathy stock. Buy the stock of the company that is *actually* moving higher.

➢ Stock-splits generally bode well for investors.

➢ The market never discounts the same thing twice.

➤ *"Get inside information from the president and you will probably lose half of your money. If you get it from the chairman of the board, you will lose all of it."*

— Jim Rogers

➤ If investments are keeping you awake at night — sell down to the sleeping point.

➤ In a correction, the market goes down much faster than it goes up as panicked investors stampede to get out.

➢ Patience is more important than market timing.

➢ Cut your losses and let your profits run. Most average investors do just the opposite by cutting their profits and letting their losses run. They grab at the first inkling of a profit and then hold on to their losers hoping to 'at least get even,' while sinking deeper in the hole.

➢ Wall Street is motivated primarily by two emotions — fear and greed.

➢ Stocks with low cash-flow multiples typically outperform those with high multiples by more than 4-to-1.

➤ Best tip the market will ever give you —
   never answer a margin call.

➤ Avoid the stock of a company that just
   announced the move to a fancy new
   corporate headquarters building.

➤ *"Every investor should be prepared financially and psychologically for the possibility of poor short-term results. For example, in the 1973-1974 decline the investor would have lost money on paper, but if he'd held on and stuck with the approach, he would have recouped in 1975-1976 and gotten his 15 percent average return for the five-year period."*

— Benjamin Graham

➤ *"Any man who is a bear on the future of this country will go broke."*

— J. P. Morgan

➤ *"There are two times in a man's life when he should not speculate — when he can't afford it and when he can."*

— Mark Twain

➤ Never make a decision to sell
on Sunday morning.

➤ Avoid the roller coaster of worry by *not* checking your stock prices in the paper every day. How often do you check on the value of your home?

➤ Don't buy a stock just because it has a low
P/E — it's probably low for a reason.

➤ Successful investors have the courage to
buy when others are selling and the
courage to sell when others are buying.

➢ The trend is your friend.

➢ Be greedy when others are fearful.

➢ Market timing is a losing proposition.

➤ *"Timidity prompted by past failures causes investors to miss the most important bull markets."*

— Walter Schloss

➢ Staying out of the market can be costly.
During the bull market of August 1982
thru August 1987, the S&P 500 went up
26.3% a year on average. However, anyone
who sat out the 40 best days of those five
years would have realized an annual return
of only 4.3%. Sitting out just 10 of the best
days out of the 1,276 trading days cut the
annualized return by 8% to 18.3%.

➤ Turn-around situations rarely turn.

➤ To make a small fortune buying options —
start out with a large fortune.

➤ The odds are greater that the market will
continue in the same direction it is going,
than that it will reverse directions.

➤ No tree grows to the sky.

➤ Buy when you can't find a bull.

➤ Nobody ever lost money taking a profit.

➢ Bull markets have no resistance — bear markets have no support.

➢ A stock that goes down 50% and comes back 50% — is *still* down 25%.

➤ *"You can think more objectively with cash in your stock account than you can if you are worrying about a stock that has lost money for you. There are other securities where your chance of recouping your loss could be far greater."*

— William O'Neil

➤ Not to decide is to decide.

➤ Watch the company — not the stock price.

➤ High-yield growth stock — an oxymoron.

➤ *"Nobody can predict interest rates, the future direction of the economy or the stock market. Dismiss all such forecasts and concentrate on what's actually happening to the companies in which you've invested."*

— Peter Lynch

➢ Timing isn't everything! If a hypothetical, hapless investor had managed to totally *mistime* the market for the past 16 years by investing $10,000 at the peak of the market each year, his $160,000 investment still would have grown by 238% to $540,000 — far surpassing money-market or T-bill rates.

"Think about the compounding effect of your
dividend reinvestment program — it helps."

➤ Never hold on to a loser just to collect the dividends.

➤ If you made money — you invested, if you lost money — you speculated.

➤ Patience neutralizes risk.

➤ Never dip into capital.

➤ Wall Street hates surprises.

➤ The market tends to have a sell-off every fall.

➤ *"Some extremely sharp investment advisors can get you in at the bottom of the market. Some extremely sharp ones can get you out at the top. They are never the same people."*

— Gary North

➤ Stocks are never too high to begin buying — or too low to begin selling.

> The stock market is a barometer, not a thermometer.

> A company's earnings *estimates* tend to impact its stock price more dramatically than *actual* earnings results.

➢ Human nature is always in conflict with successful investing.

➢ As a bear market begins to bottom out, buy the stock that has gone down the *most* and the stock that has gone down the *least*.

➤ *"Unless you can watch your stock holdings decline by 50% without becoming panic-stricken, you should not be in the stock market."*

— Warren Buffett

➤ *"The smart, steely-nerved investor will shrug off mini-crashes."*

— Mark Hurlbert

➤ *"The worse a situation becomes, the less it takes to turn it around — and the bigger the upside."*

— George Soros

➤ There's more anxiety in being *out* of a bull market than being *in* a bear market.

➢ Growth will bail you out — if you live long enough.

➢ Never sell based on a war scare — in the past, the initial shock has always been followed by a recovery.

➤ *"You never grow poor taking profits,
and you don't grow rich taking a
four-point spread in a bull market."*

— Jesse Livermore

➢ *"Fear causes you to panic and sell at the bottom, while greed motivates you to buy near the top."*

— Stan Weinstein

➤ Don't hold on to a mistake.

➤ Buy when doom and gloom is everywhere.

➤ Selling right is half solved by buying right.

➤ The out-of-favor stock of a good company will eventually come back strong.

➤ When you hear that everybody's buying a particular stock, remember — just as many are selling.

➤ *"If you take the time to choose only the stocks of great companies, you will still be hurt when the market pulls back. But you will be able to sleep easy in the knowledge that your stocks will lead the next bull charge up the mountain."*

— Stephen Leeb

➤ The key to creating wealth —
compound interest over time.

➤ Your first loss is your best loss.

➤ Always buy and sell 'at the market.'

➤ Take windfall profits when you have them.

➤ *"There is no evidence that profitable market timing can be done on a consistent basis. But there is sufficient evidence to suggest that market timing involves extreme risk of being out of the market at the wrong time."*

— Bob Anslow

➤ Two things cause a stock to move — the expected and the unexpected.

➤ Companies repurchasing their stock in the market typically has a positive effect on share price.

➤ *"Money is made by discounting the obvious and betting on the unexpected."*

— George Soros

➤ *"In investing money, the amount of investment you want should depend on whether you want to eat well or sleep well."*

— J. Kennfield Morley

➤ Before selling, wait for the worry
to actually happen.

➤ *"Forget technical analysis. It is not knowable from what a stock did last month or last year, how it will do next month or next year."*

— John Train

➢ Never throw good money after bad.

➢ The stock market is a polling machine.

➢ Don't be in a hurry to take your profits.

➢ Big drops in the market are almost always great buying opportunities.

➢ When the stock market makes the front page of the newspapers and everybody is talking stocks — the bull market is just about over.

➤ *"The time to buy securities is when the media is so full of doom that your trembling hand can scarcely hold the telephone to call your broker with a buy order."*

— James Michaels

➤ Buy on weakness — sell on strength.

➤ When there's blood in the streets — buy.

➤ Be a trend follower — not a trend fighter.

➤ *"It was the steady investors who kept their heads when the stock market tanked in October 1987, and then saw the value of their holdings eventually recover and continue to produce attractive returns."*

— Burton Malkiel

➤ Don't be afraid to buy a stock making new highs. A stock at a new high of 50 must *keep making* new highs at 55, 57, and 59 on the way to 60.

"You have become a very rich man. I wish more of my
clients had your investment philosophy, Mr. VanWinkle."

➤ *"I found dollar-cost averaging to be a successful overall strategy as long as one concentrated on stock purchases of companies that demonstrated consistent earnings and dividend growth. Dollar-cost averaging can be disastrous if you fail to purchase stocks that are continually increasing in value."*

— George Connell

➤ Don't swim against the tide.

➤ Avoid stocks in fad industries.

➤ Insider buying is usually a positive signal.

➢ An extraordinarily high dividend rate may indicate an eventual dividend *cut*.

➢ Beware of companies who hold their annual meetings at inopportune times and in out-of-the-way places.

➢ Winners keep on winning.

➤ To be a successful market timer you would have to be right twice, when you buy and when you sell. To be right the first time, you have a 50% chance — to be right on both sides of the trade, you have a 25% chance.

➤ Price is what you pay — value is what you get.

➤ Most stocks fluctuate 50% from low to high each year.

➢ Every time a trade is made —
somebody was wrong.

➤ *"The hidden trap of reinvesting dividends is reinvestment in a poor fund. If you don't want to sell your existing shares of a poor fund ... at least stop buying more! Call the fund and instruct it to start sending you the dividends and distributions in cash. Then channel that money into a superior fund."*

— Jay Shabacker

➤ *"A bull market is illogical, irrational and you can't diagnose how far it is going to go — but it always ends. Then you have a bear market, and during that you can usually tell the bottom."*

— Roy Neuberger

➤ Long shots rarely pay off.

➤ Sell your worst performing stock first.

➤ There will be a bear market — there always is.

➤ Companies growing at greater than 50%
   per year cannot keep it up.

➤ As an investor, don't permit yourself to be
   sidetracked by negative rumors or the possibility of quick profits from a speculation.

➤ *"In the book of things people more often do wrong than right, investing must certainly top the list, followed closely by wallpapering and eating artichokes."*

— Robert Klein

➢ *"Far more money has been lost by investors preparing for corrections or trying to anticipate corrections than has been lost in corrections themselves."*

— Peter Lynch

➤ Most investors never learn from their past mistakes.

➤ Short selling is risky — but certainly not un-American.

➤ Doing nothing, while a substantial profit disappears just to avoid paying taxes, is folly.

➤ The first time a company reduces its earnings estimate is bad — the second time is usually disastrous.

> ➤ *"An investment strategy is not worth much if you constantly change due to a lack of underlying confidence or comfort. This is the difference between investing and playing the market."*
>
> — Peter Skirkanich

➤ Better to pay a fair price for a good company than a cheap price for a loser.

➤ CDs and treasury bills are not investments — just places to park your money while you decide where to invest.

➢ Economists have correctly
predicted nine out of the last
five recessions.

➤ *"A loss never bothers me after I take it.
I forget it. But being wrong — not taking
the loss — that is what does damage to
the pocketbook and to the soul."*

— Jesse Livermore

➤ Go the way the market goes.

➤ The more confused the investor, the more absolute certainty he will demand from his financial advisor.

➤ Famous last words — "This time it's going to be different."

➤ Resist the temptation to 'invest' in new issues — most will ultimately be losers.

➤ *"A small loss, when realized, becomes an opportunity for profit elsewhere. It gives you the chance to turn a liability into an asset, instead of just sitting there praying that your old stock will come back."*

— Martin Zweig

➢ To create long term wealth — be an investor, not a speculator.

➤ Only speculate with what you can afford
to lose.

➤ Money is made when you buy stocks on
weakness and stocks in distress — not
when they are in high demand.

➤ Understand the magic of compound interest!
If you received $1,000 a day for 30 days you
would end up with $30,000. If, on the other
hand, you received one penny the first day, then
double the previous day's total the second day
and so on for the entire 30 days, you would end
up with an astonishing $10,737,418.23. Half-
way into the 30 days you would only have had
$327.67, but does it ever pick up steam over the
second half. Moral: *Reinvest* all dividends, interest and capital gains distributions.

➢ If the idea is right, eighths and quarters won't matter.

➢ When investing for 10 years or longer, there isn't much difference between load and no-load mutual funds.

➤ *"Don't wait until the time or the market is just right to start investing — start now. The best time to plant an oak tree was 20 years ago — the second best time is now."*

— James Stowers

➢ Average up — not down.

➢ Markets usually anticipate.

➢ A stock does not know you own it.

➤ If the industry leader is overvalued, don't buy the dogs.

➤ The best defense in the face of an impending market correction is owning great stocks.

"Wait a second, I *am* getting a read
on the emerging global markets.".

➢ A rising tide raises all ships.

➢ Never buy just to get a dividend.

➢ Buy stocks when the market is depressed.

> Don't panic when the market seems to be falling apart.

➤ *"One of the best rules anybody can learn about investing is to do nothing, absolutely nothing, unless there is something to do. Most people always have to be playing — they always have to be doing something."*

— Jim Rogers

➤ Time is the friend of stocks — the enemy of bonds.

➤ The Rule of 72 determines how long it will take to double your money — divide the rate of return into 72.

➤ Markets must reverse.

➤ In a bull market, be bullish.

➤ High risk seldom equals high return.

➢ *"The hard-to-accept great paradox in the stock market is that what seems too high and risky to the majority usually goes higher and what seems low and cheap usually goes lower."*

— William O'Neil

➤ *"Prices have no memory, and yesterday has nothing to do with tomorrow. Every day starts out fifty-fifty. Yesterday's price discounted everything yesterday."*

— Adam Smith

➤ The Dow has never reached its inflation-adjusted peak set in 1966.

➤ Investors love to talk about their stocks going up — but not a peep when they're going down.

> ➤ Don't buy a stock just because it's low — or sell just because it's high.

> ➤ Small company stocks move faster than large company stocks — up *and* down.

➤ *"If you expect to continue to purchase
stocks throughout your life, you should
welcome price declines as a way to add
stocks more cheaply to your portfolio."*

— Warren Buffett

➤ *"Bears don't live on Park Avenue."*
— Bernard Baruch

➤ *"The only way to make money buying overpriced stocks is if they become more overpriced."*
— Michael Metz

➢ Buying a stock trading *above* its 200-day moving average tends to have positive results.

➢ Cyclical stocks tend to lead the market in economic recoveries.

➢ Stocks have outperformed bonds in each of the nine decades of this century except one — the 1930s.

➢ *"Your success in investing will depend in part on your character and guts, and in part on your ability to realize, at the height of ebullience and the depth of despair alike, that this, too, shall pass."*

—John Bogle

➤ *"Investors repeatedly jump ship on a good strategy just because it hasn't worked so well lately, and, almost invariably, abandon it at precisely the wrong time."*

— David Dreman

➤ A company's first earnings disappointment
won't be the last.

➤ Low inflation and low interest rates usually
result in a strong stock market.

➢ Never buy a stock that won't go *up* in a bull market.

➢ Never sell a stock that won't go *down* in a bear market.

➤ *"The market is like a train sitting on the tracks. You can see the direction it's heading but you cannot dictate the time of departure. Those investors who put the market on a timetable not only become frustrated but end up making foolish moves. Instead, get on the train, sit back, and enjoy the scenery."*

— Roger Engemann

➤ *"Everyone has the brain power to make money in stocks — not everyone has the stomach. If you are susceptible to selling everything in a panic, you ought to avoid stocks and stock mutual funds altogether."*

— Peter Lynch

➢ An investor's worst enemy is not the stock market — but oneself.

➢ The 'new high list' will do better in the subsequent six months than the 'new low list' will.

➤ The bottom is always 10% below your worst case expectation.

➤ Don't panic if your stock has a sharp down-turn lasting for days or weeks — it can and has happened to even great stocks.

➤ *"The decision to buy a stock with dynamic potential in an uptrend may be more important in the final analysis than when you buy it."*

— Gerald Loeb

➤ You can't control the market —
but you can control your reaction
to it.

➢ Buy low, sell high.

➢ Buy high, sell higher.

➢ What you don't own can't hurt you.

➢ *"When unemployment is rising, buy stocks. When unemployment is falling, avoid stocks."*

— Stephen Leeb

➢ *"A prospectus is not designed to help investors, it is designed to disclose legal requirements."*

— Michael Lipper

> Time is the most important tool of the intelligent investor.

➤ Don't buck the trend — your trade won't be the one that turns the market around.

➤ Be critical when reading an annual report and pay special attention to the footnotes.

➤ *"The worse you feel, usually because the news is bad, the safer the market is. The better you feel, usually because the news is good, the closer you are to a top."*

— John Train

➤ *"Don't try to buy at the bottom and sell at the top. This can't be done — except by liars."*

— Bernard Baruch

➤ *"If the job has been correctly done when a common stock is purchased, the time to sell it is — almost never."*

— Philip Fisher

"I'd like to invest in a nice, honest, wholesome company that makes *obscene* profits."

➤ *"The serious investor knows that
among the many signposts that point
to corporate and investment growth,
a rising dividend trend is perhaps
the most significant."*

— Geraldine Weiss

> ➤ When three or more insiders are buying —
>   follow them.

> ➤ Over the long term, low P/E stocks will
>   outperform high P/E stocks.

➤ January tends to set the tone for the rest of the market year.

➤ Stocks always seem to rise on the day before a holiday — any holiday.

➤ *"Don't assume that the high price at which a stock may be selling in relation to earnings is necessarily an indication that further growth in those earnings has largely been already discounted in the price."*

— Philip Fisher

➤ *"If your stock goes up — buy more. You don't care how big the position gets as part of your portfolio. If you get it right, then build."*

— George Soros

➢ Buy on the rumor — sell on the news.

➢ The stock market is a two-way street.

➢ Over the long term the market goes up.

➤ Don't even try to predict the short-term direction of the stock market.

➤ Never use limit orders when buying or selling — they usually cause you to miss the market.

➢ *"October. This is one of the peculiarly dangerous months to speculate in stocks. The others are July, January, September, April, November, May, March, June, December, August and February."*

— Mark Twain

➤ *"The only way to make money in the stock market is to get in and stay with it."*

— Tony Gray

➤ *"I regard market timing as the investment management business' answer to the Tooth Fairy."*

— Roger Kirby

➢ Portfolio diversification makes up
for investor ignorance.

➤ Don't follow the crowd — it's usually wrong.

➤ Major market moves tend to be dictated by monetary policies and interest rates set by the Federal Reserve.

➤ *"The investor with a portfolio of sound stocks should expect their prices to fluctuate and should neither be concerned by sizable declines nor become excited by sizable advances."*

— Benjamin Graham

➤ You won't outsmart the market — for very long.

➤ U.S. stocks make up only one-third of the world's stock market.

➢ Never check stock prices on Friday — it could spoil your weekend.

> ➤ Nobody can accurately predict short-term market movements.

> ➤ The stock of companies experiencing rapid earnings growth *will* escalate over time.

➤ *"If you could just eliminate the worst 10% of all stocks and choose even randomly from the rest, you would beat the market."*

— Martin Zweig

➤ *"Avoid buying stock funds close to the end of the year. Stock funds typically make a single set of capital gains and income distributions each year, normally in late December. Owners of stock funds have to pay taxes on those distributions, even if they have only just bought shares."*

— Jonathan Clements